BEHIND BARRES

The Mystique of Masterly Teaching

BEHIND BARRES

THE MYSTIQUE OF MASTERLY TEACHING

by
JOSEPH GALE

DANCE HORIZONS • NEW YORK

ISBN 0-87127-115-X

Library of Congress Catalog Card Number 79 - 56900

Printed in the United States of America

Dance Horizons, 1801 East 26th Street, Brooklyn, N.Y. 11229

To my wife

For good and sundry reasons the author
expresses gratitude to Agnes de Mille for aid,
example, and wisdom; A. J. Pischl, publisher and
friend, whose patience shall henceforth be
legend; Joseph C. Koenenn, arts and leisure
editor of *Newsday,* with whom, in a sense, it all
began; and Susan Olive, transcriber
extraordinaire.

'Diaghilev dies, Pavlova dies asking for her Swan dress, and there is a terrifying silence, but in all the dancing schools, classes continue as if there were still something left for which to live. After a few false starts the broken threads are once more gathered together, and our art enjoys a glorious renaissance.'

ARNOLD HASKELL
Balletomania Then & Now

CONTENTS

◇

◇

PREFACE

◇

THIS IS A STUDY of that rare and precious artificial resource, the master teacher of ballet—a definition we shall have more to say about later on.

For several reasons we restricted our search to the United States and selected a good many more candidates than appear in this book. Choosing so-called master teachers may seem like an arbitrary exercise, but the choice needs to be defensible, after all, and the individuals who consented (in some surprise and bemusement) not only appeared on my list but were among the first suggestions of more than a dozen authoritative and respected dancers, choreographers, and other teachers.

This is not to say that there are not many more master teachers out there, some with coteries and reputations within the craft, many others with little more than their names and the assurance of an eternal reputation constructed on words-of-mouth. It was possible to select a relative few here and to hope that other writers might awaken to the realization that the countless barre-ed and mirrored rooms from sea to shining sea do not awaken to life until the teachers enter them.

It once was said, "The choreographer is king!" That is a basic truth; and some choreographers are great teachers as well—but perhaps only of their own ballets. Yet choreographers are mute without human clay to work with, and the best of that material is kneaded and shaped by other royalty who know that they transmit a hallowed tradition and that their obligation is as much to the past as to the future.

The personae of this volume recognize that they are at the top of their profession. But by and large they accept the fact without fanfare and seem content, or resigned, to be accepted as such within the narrow confines of the ballet world. Thus it would seem that when approached to speak of their work and methods for the appreciation of a larger audience they would accept the opportunity without ado, perhaps even with alacrity.

Hardly so. One teacher acquiesced after exhaustive bona fides and guarantees were established, only to decline within 24 hours. Another defeated me by attrition after a year's unique correspondence that itself may one day furnish a footnote to ballet history. One or two declined to reply to repeated inquiries. And still another did accept, only to backpedal in the following week with fancier footwork than ever was seen in the studio.

Thus the individuals here represent the distillation of a search. They proved to be gracious, charming, helpful, understanding, and patient. They were reluctant only about particulars of their private lives—and that one must grant. About their philosophies and methods they were quite open. Their sole interest was to transmit the heritage of the past, to animate unformed bodies with the splendor of tradition, and to kindle sparks of greatness within the already talented.

Here, then, are some of the cream among master teachers today, the bearers of the torch, the inhabitants of a rarefied stratum of ballet society. Without them and their colleagues the art of ballet might still be a pleasure of the French court.

◇

INTRODUCTION

◇

THERE ARE THOUSANDS of ballet teachers actively at work in the United States today, which is not unusual in a country that is indisputably the dance capital of the world. Few communities of appreciable population are without one or more dance studios. In general, many of these lack distinction in the sense of being temples of dance in which boys and girls are trained for professional careers—although the ablest graduates are indeed fed into the regional ballet system or sent upward into momentous auditions.

Some schools, and the instructors who work there, offer little more than a pretense at art. Some are run by people who themselves never danced professionally. The quality of teaching is mundane and pedestrian, and if anywhere there is a spark it will ignite spontaneously in the student, without benefit of teacher.

Most ballet training is of a higher order than this, fortunately, with goals more clearly perceived, the teaching more profound, and a sense of dedication directly, even if tenuously, linked with tradition.

The very finest schools and teachers are perforce found in the cities, where they are attached to major performing companies or are independent of them but linked by symbiosis and a bond of artistic interest that transcends the five basic positions. This is not to say that there are no exceptions, and that here and there, especially in the rapidly developing university programs, extremely fine, thoughtful, and disciplined teaching is not to be found.

But the best teachers are in the urban centers probably because that is where the opportunity is and where students with purpose gravitate. Here are the concentrations of teachers who feel that life has amply repaid them if they are able to discover and develop one or two or three superb dancers. And among these are a few teachers who have been elevated to Olympus by the word-of-mouth of students who take lessons from them and performers who coach with them. These are the master teachers—a designation as ephemeral as prima ballerina assoluta, which means little in coin of the realm but which, in the tight little world of ballet, means that these are the paramount inheritors of a sacred tradition whose pioneers fought, starved, and endured so that the art might survive in the glow of their utter belief.

Some people themselves use the phrase "Master Teacher" in their advertisements, and one wonders at their audacity. Perhaps, indeed, they are. But none of the individuals you will meet here advertise personally, so far as I know, nor do they need to. Their worth is above rubies, and they are handed over from student to student like icons.

What, after all, are master teachers? What value do they have that any good, competent, professional teacher does not? And today, when the language of movement has long been codified, when all the steps and exercises have been set down and there seems nothing more left to do, why master teachers?

The term is difficult to define. We know what a ballerina is (at least some of us do; the word is among the most abused in the language); we know what a prima ballerina is; and when the addition of assoluta originated under the tsars we sensed in our blood what that meant. Well, the difference between a prima and an assoluta is the difference between a fine teacher and a master teacher.

Those tacitly considered by their associates and students to be master teachers impart more than steps and combinations. They are more than sharp-eyed in the classroom. That they exert discipline is taken for granted. That they know the rules and regimen of the studio is assumed, and that they turn beginners into intermediates, and intermediates into advanceds, goes without saying.

What sets them apart is a certain devotion to heritage, a kinship with history, an unaspirated acquiescence in the mandate of their progenitors to hand down the torch rekindled by their own fire. These are the men and women who toil unsung, who never appear in front of the curtain unless they are also choreographers, who seldom make much money, whose redemption lies not merely in the bodies of others, but in their souls as well. They are drudges, but angels too, and whether they know it or not they respond every teaching day to the far-off call of Vestris and Blasis and Cecchetti. Most master teachers would be startled if accosted by such devotions, but neither would they absolutely deny them.

Enrico Cecchetti (1850–1928) termed the teacher of ballet a "book of the dance" and once said to Serge Lifar, "Up to now I have been this book, and for you I am an 'open book.' You read in it, and now it is up to you to open this book for the benefit of others in order that our beloved art may not perish."*

Beloved art. It is this reverence for the elevation of the spirit that some teachers dimly perceive, but master teachers accept like breathing. In the formative years of modern group dance—say, in the middle of the eighteenth century—such folk dances as we know of sprang from the individual's bond with earth and sky, and even the social dancing of the court was a stylized expression of the impulse to move with some degree of pattern toward a higher plane. The ladies and gentlemen of society might have derided such a notion, but we can understand now that the elements were there.

By the time the great Jean Georges Noverre (1727–1810) came upon the scene the die was cast. As a dancer, innovator, and yes, master teacher, he helped shape the thing that was to become ballet as we know it. The landmark teachers who continued the tradition, the open book, each adding and refining, stand out like beacons: Gaspare Angiolini (1731–1803); the Viganos—Onorato (1739–1811) and Salvatore (1769–1821); the magnificent August Vestris (1760–1842); the celebrated Taglionis—Filippo (1777–1871), Salvatore (1789–1869), and Paolo (1808–1884); the fundamental Carlo Blasis (1795–1878); his disciple, Giovanni Lepri (1830?–1890?); the Cecchettis—Cesare (1821–1899) and Enrico; and Agrippina Vaganova (1879–1951). There were others, of course.

Today there would not seem to be much more that is discoverable about ballet. Are there steps we yet know nothing about? No, but as the range of physical prowess lengthens and broadens there are different combinations of steps. Is there anything choreographically new under the sun? Not as such, but with the rapprochement in this generation of ballet and contemporary dance limitless vistas of unfamiliar creation are uncovered.

As far as anyone can tell, it would seem that the age of exploration has yielded to the age of experiment and development. This is a debatable point, however. Some theorists and master teachers, if they took time to think about it at all, would argue that the beauty of ballet is that as dancers' bodies become ever more refined, and as techniques of using them become more finely attuned to possibilities, the art of ballet is in perpetual dissolve from one kinaesthetic montage to another—and so, never static, ever changing.

Whether they think consciously in such terms, master teachers are keepers of the flame, guarantors of the purity of that vessel which is the body of classical ballet, the founding stone, the primer without which the language would collapse upon itself. And so the ABC's are retold every day, the catechism of classical ballet mounted afresh in classes from one coast to the other. The morning *barre* yields to the noontime *plié* and *étendre* and *tourner,* segueing into the afternoon *élancé* and *glissade* and the evening *relevé,* the soaring flight that caps the meaning of everything, the resolving of all differences.

And in the process the true master of teaching stiffens the spine of the boy or girl sweating at the barre, kindles a flame in the eye and causes a quarter-inch lift to an already proud head. Or erases from the practiced performer an error unknowingly assumed, or gives as a gift an old idea now rethought. How? One is hard put to analyze. A look has been known to do it, a new intonation of familiar instructions, words of wisdom (though not many of those), a reminiscence. But the magic is done, and the moment in time is enshrined forever. All good teachers do all of these, and for their students it is merely part of the learning process. Master teachers do them, and by some strange alchemy the clouds part and a thought stands revealed.

*Serge Lifar, "Cecchetti—A Memoir," *The Dancing Times,* January 1929.

Left: Margaret Craske as a dancer in her twenties. This is one of the few photographs of Craske from the early years. Nearly all her possessions, including photos, programs and other records, were lost in the Blitz of London during World War II.

Below: Craske with Nadia Nerina of The Royal Ballet and Ted Shawn, founder of Jacob's Pillow, during a rehearsal pause at The Pillow in October, 1967. Dancer at rear is unidentified. Photo by John Lindquist.

Right: Craske today on her high stool usually alongside the rehearsal piano in the Manhattan School of Dance.

A NONDANCING VISITOR to Margaret Craske's apartment one day, in the act of making his departure, illustrated a farewell remark with a mock port de bras.

Quickly and without expression Craske corrected the position of his outflung hand.

The typical gesture indicated that, though perfectly willing to jest, Craske insisted with British imperturbability and a sense of fitness that it be a *beau geste.*

It is the same manner in which she conducts her classes. Though she herself, ensconced on a high stool alongside the piano, is fairly immobile, her eyes are not. The studio in which she teaches at the Manhattan School of Dance is irregular in shape, yet there is no escape from her notice or her dry, nonaccusatory wit in even the farthest reach of that room. Craske neither skewers nor impales. Her attitude says: "Come now, you really know better than that. Let's do it correctly, shall we?"

From Craske emanates the immense authority of the weary. Her experience is encyclopedic. Yet she is patient and gentle, with a matter-of-factness laced by humor that allows for foibles, but not absurdity.

Craske was born in Norfolk, England, in 1892, "not a good year for professional dancing in the British Isles. And I never wanted to do anything else, not then. And even later, the music halls were where it was at. Ah, the English music halls! I learned so much about the theater from the music halls, almost more than I did from the theater."

Ballet won a grudging imprimatur in England with the visits of the Diaghilev Ballets Russes in 1911 and through the twenties, "but before that people just didn't take up dancing. It wasn't the thing to do. I mean, you just didn't take up ballet."

Craske, who was as determined then as now, did. "I had done some dancing at school, ordinary dancing, plenty of it, and I wanted to go to London. There was a certain amount of resistance on the part of my family. Not much. They were very decent about it. The idea wasn't popular, but they gave me some money and let me go. I studied with a woman in Hampshire first."

Enrico Cecchetti had opened a studio in London in 1918, and Craske took class with him for five years, appearing during this period for two seasons with the Diaghilev Ballets Russes, one of the first English dancers to do so. She became a disciple of the Cecchetti method and worked actively in her younger days for its dissemination. In 1924, assisted by Mabel Ryan, another Cecchetti student, she opened the Craske-Ryan School in London and offered various styles of dance, even Spanish, as well as ballet. The school's fortunes fluctuated with the times and with Craske's repeated absences in India on what she was to consider a higher calling, and it closed finally on the eve of World War II.

Meanwhile, as early as 1920, Craske's pedagogical interests became evident with the publication of a study, *The Theory and Practice of Allegro in Classical Ballet,* co-authored with Cyril Beaumont, the dance critic and historian. A similar title related to advanced allegro, written with Friderica Derra de Moroda, another widely respected dance historian, was published in 1956.

Craske continued to dance during the 1920s, getting her music hall exposure with Ninette de Valois and a small touring group, but this aspect of her career was phasing out under the more desirable persuasions of teaching and choreography. Then, also, she had injured her left Achilles tendon—the bane of so many female dancers—and although her foot healed, rheumatism followed and stayed.

Craske choreographed considerably for the Carl Rosa Opera Company in England and for many London shows. She followed de Valois into the Sadler's Wells Ballet Company as a guest instructor and continued her franchise with the then-new Cecchetti Society, founded by the master in 1922 at the instigation of Beaumont, who thought it a good idea if

Cecchetti's English pupils became known to one another. Later, when Cecchetti returned to Italy, the society's purpose was broadened to include preserving the master's teachings for posterity. In 1928 Craske visited Johannesburg, Durban, and Cape Town as a representative of the society, which as a result of her work established a Cecchetti Committee for South Africa.

Craske was associated with Beaumont in the 1920s in at least one other phase of her career when they devised choreography for a number of dances and formed the Beaucraske Dancers. As John Percival, the English critic, recalls:

"The Beaucraske Dancers rehearsed their repertory and finally thought themselves ready to appear in public. Beaumont secured for them an audition with the theatrical agent who booked Diaghilev's company. Things did not go well, however, and were not much helped when one girl was given a glass of brandy to steady her nerves. She was to play the Bull in a little ballet based on bull-fighting; when she put on the head which formed part of her costume, she became dizzy and could not see, with results better imagined then described.

"No engagement followed, and the little group broke up, Beaumont and Craske dividing the costumes between them."*

If Cecchetti and Beaumont were important to Craske's professional life, Meher Baba, an Indian guru, was decisive. Craske met the teacher in 1931 and shortly after placed herself under his discipline in India. She studied with him there again in 1935 and still further in 1939, when she stayed for seven years. In between, while still serving with Sadler's Wells, Craske would meet her instructor in various parts of Europe; but after the 1935 absence of about six months, de Valois declined to let her rejoin the company.

"Ninette was very nice about it, but she said 'We simply can't have this, love.' It is true that they had to find replacements for me, but on the other hand, I never had a contract with them. It all just happened, and they just got used to seeing me around.

"I had been looking for something all my life, and I found it with Meher Baba. It was, quite simply, love. I'm not talking about human love, but a kind of love that you can call God, if you like. It's a very spiritual quality, and it may have affected my later teaching. I certainly don't teach with hate. What I learned from Meher Baba is deep within me still."

Craske returned to England in 1946, the year of Ballet Theatre's first season in London. She had lost nearly all her possessions in the Blitz, including documents, photographs, and records. At the suggestion of Antony Tudor, to whom Craske had been recommended as a teacher as early as 1928, Ballet Theatre invited Craske to come to the United States as ballet mistress and teacher. Since Meher Baba had earlier advised her to take up her life in America, Craske went. She remained a luminary behind the scenes at Ballet Theatre even after 1950, when the company and the Metropolitan Opera combined to form a joint school at the Metropolitan Opera House.

After Ballet Theatre brought that association to an end, Craske stayed on until 1966 as assistant director of the opera ballet school, also teaching at the Juilliard School. In 1968 thoughts of retirement were interrupted by Robert Ossorio, who asked if she would consider transferring to his Manhattan School of Dance, just then being formed, as a teacher and director of ballet instruction.

" 'Well,' I thought, 'that sounds nice.' So I did."

Craske's pedagogy has touched the lives of some of ballet's most memorable people, among them Gerald Arpino, Melissa Hayden, Loren Hightower, Nora Kaye, Hugh Laing, Mary Skeaping, Glen Tetley, Peggy van Praagh, and Sallie Wilson.

The Cecchetti method, a difficult and severe regimen of unvarying daily exercise based on an understanding of principles rather than on imitation of movement, is seldom anywhere taught in its entirety these days. Large chunks of Cecchetti are, however, or are adapted to modern ways. Cecchetti's contributions, and the soundness of his rules and theories, informed a generation of the famous, from Pavlova to Markova, from Nijinsky to Dolin.

The rules are, unwittingly or not, part of innumerable syllabuses. Ballet teaching these days is lodged with the many, more than with the few, and thus is more eclectic than ever before. The international style reigns. Even Craske no longer exactly follows Cecchetti's table of daily exercises, although this canon is the foundation of her lore. In an article written a year after Cecchetti's death, Craske, imbued with his ideals, advised students that dancing was closely associated with music, sculpture, and drama and that they could profitably spend hours in museums contemplating the feeling and rhythm in sculpture as associated with the flow of movement in the studio.

Today, restfully in place on her director's stool, clad comfortably in oversize moccasins, her eagle eyes focused, Craske slips into the role of disciplinarian with the practice of ages. Her lookout is entirely for the benefit of her students, for as she observes, a foot placed in error means that the hip is out of place, and if the hip is out of place the whole delicately balanced structure that is the body may eventually be harmed. Besides, she says, a student who cannot or will not learn correctly, and will not strive besides, does a disservice to everyone concerned.

"I do not give in," she says. "I never give in. I insist on their doing things the right way—the only way, as long as they're with me. If they leave the school because I happen to prevail, that's all right. I want my students to take their work seriously, as if they planned to follow professional careers in the dance even when they don't. I do not like turning them out of the school, but I will if I must."

Yet Craske is patient and will accommodate a struggling student for as long as a year before deciding. It is just as often a hurrah as a goodbye.

Long ago under the guidance of Meher Baba she relinquished the trap of personal ego, and she teaches with a selflessness that has endeared her to generations of students. She makes light of her years, yet she is aware of the toll upon her strength, which she is careful to conserve. She no longer teaches privately, for instance, because of the tension involved, except now and then "a first-class artist who needs to brush up on something." And if an otherwise talented student experiences difficulty in mastering an exercise or combination, Craske will ask another student to demonstrate the correct way rather than hold up the class to work out the difficulty herself.

Craske is strict, but she is not an autocrat. The glint of a girl's earring that would upset anyone else does not unduly bother her. Banter between students perspiring at the barre is generally overlooked if it is brief and inaudible. Craske is confident of every eye, every ear attuned to her vibrations, every pair of legs set to spring.

She is filled with a sort of resigned amusement, in class, and with wit as dry as kindling. Flagrant violations draw proper rebukes, but anything less will elicit a comment, disguised as a common plea by virtue of tone alone, and an almost invisible twitch of the lip.

"Get your groundwork first. This is advanced work."

"Please learn it. It's an elementary step."

"Turn your hips out. Turn your knees!"

"It is not done with the leg up."

"You have to go up, up. This is a big jump, so you have to go up."

"These things are all very subtle. It's not a huge turnaround, you know."

"Perhaps it'll be better if you don't care what you're doing."

And the threnody, repeated a thousand times:

"Get it right!"

*John Percival, "When Cyril Beaumont Formed a Ballet Company," *Dance and Dancers,* December 1961.

LEON DANIELIAN

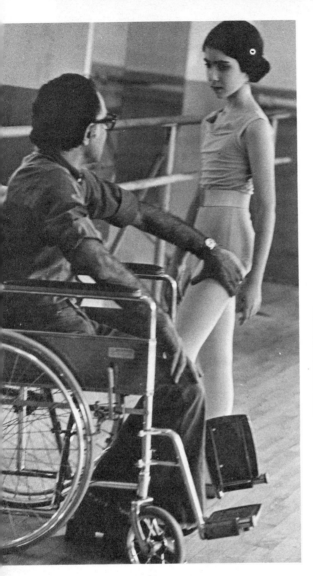

Above: Leon Danielian, former director of, now consultant of, the American Ballet Theatre School, in class after his first operation in 1971 when he was still largely confined to a wheelchair. Photo by Chas Ray.

Right: Soon after his third and last operation, Danielian was able at last to stand without pain and conduct class in total command of his body once again. Photo by Myron Papiz.

Above: In Ruth Page's *Frankie and Johnny*, 1947.

Right: With Alexandra Danilova in *Gaîté Parisienne*.

Below: With Nina Novak in *Coppélia*, 1955.

Photos by Fred Fehl.

Left: Danielian in class at the American Ballet Theatre School, 1967.

Below: With Ruthanna Boris in *Coppélia*. Photo by Fred Fehl.

Right: Danielian's face reveals the exaltation with which he teaches. Photo by Sigrid Estrada.

I

N BALLET STUDIOS throughout the land there is a convention whereby, after an hour or so of pure dictatorship, the session ends with a "Thank you" from the teacher and the paradox of applause from perspiring and exhausted students who have every reason to hate.

The handclapping says something about reaction to discipline that the young men and women all know they need and secretly want; to what they perceive to be the quality of instruction just delivered; to their personal value of the teacher; and in a sense to the privilege of being in the hot, sweaty room of mirrors in the first place.

The applause for Leon Danielian, former director, and now consultant, of the American Ballet Theatre School, is never merely polite, rarely brief, and tends to shatter decibels—ricocheting among the walls longer than is seemly and, where men are concerned, accompanied by whistling. It is conduct appropriate for baseball, doubly startling since it refers to an enterprise far more strenuous than the national pastime, and delicate as well, and since it is love bespoken.

Love and respect for Danielian are issued at registration as part of standard equipment and shortly are confirmed at first sight. A former international *premier danseur* laid low but unconquered by osteoarthritis and surgery, Danielian teaches with enormous empathy for the individual and a high regard for humanity.

His courtesy is unfailing, his discipline tempered by it. His students are taught, shown, admonished, scolded, but all with compassion and concern. He is that rare combination, avuncular and debonair both.

Danielian is a toucher—the most circumspect. He will turn out a leg, place a pair of hips, boost a neckline with the gentlest of contacts. He will remonstrate with an erring student (though in the immediate aural vicinity only) and soften the words with a comradely pat on the arm. He is a gentleman with manners, enormously successful as a father figure. He is a consummate teacher.

The idea of teaching began to attract Danielian at the height of his career as a dancer and the outset of his career as a member of the walking wounded. Always a robust lad, Danielian nevertheless contracted blood poisoning as a boy, and that left him amenable to parental suggestion that he take to dance in order "to build myself up."

A native New Yorker, Danielian and his family moved in the early years to Atlantic Highlands, along the New Jersey shore, a bucolic community in those days, where the boy thrived on vigorous outdoor life and plenty of baseball. When Danielian came of high school age the family returned to New York for its educational advantages, and the future star, restless for continuing exercise, set out at the age of 13 in basketball shorts and sneakers for a dance class run by Seda Suny. He found that he liked it, even as the only male on the premises, and would have remained longer had not a friend persuaded him to visit the studio of Mikhail Mordkin, the great Russian dancer and former director of the Bolshoi Ballet and Mordkin Ballet.

This time Danielian arrived in his first pair of tights (maroon), entered the studio unobtrusively, lowered himself onto a couch—and knocked over the gong. It was to be the last ungraceful movement of his life.

Arthritis, which most people live with, though painfully, without markedly disrupting their lives, is a terror that confronts the dancer every day. Or a stretched metatarsal. Or a ripped Achilles tendon. Or a separation in the calf. Or bunions, corns, and the like. Bleeding feet, even, would have been a pleasure compared to the trick that fate played on Danielian.

At the age of 32 or 33, riding the crest of a brilliant career as an international star, Danielian learned that he had osteoarthritis. It was not going to get better. His left hip was starting to disintegrate, and his left leg was getting undeniably shorter. Danielian altered his choreography to place left-leg stress on the right leg (somewhat analagous to learning how to write with the other hand), but by 1958 he knew that the end of his days as a dancer was near.

A double accident decided the issue. Walking one day toward the Ballet Russe de Monte Carlo School in New York, Danielian fell on the rain-slicked sidewalk. It hurt. He walked into the studio to begin work and fell again, on his bad hip. Two years later, in 1960, he gave up dancing and began to teach at Ballet Russe and at his own establishment, the Leon Danielian School of Ballet, in White Plains, north of New York City.

Both schools closed their doors in 1966. Danielian, who had found himself overworked by the double assignment, took a week off. Then, accepting the proverbial offer he could not refuse, he became director of the American Ballet Theatre School on July 6, 1966.

Six years later he took to a wheelchair and might be there still had it not been for the urging of friends, who related a new surgical technique that would permit him to walk again. Subsequently he endured three operations which took 1½ inches off his height but not his stature. Some of the surgery took place during the time when "First Position," a film about life in a ballet school, was being made. Danielian is shown in class before and after surgery, and the delight on the faces of his students as he conducts his first class on his own two feet is one of the finer moments on the screen.

Today, Danielian divides his time between the ABT School and the Enid Knapp Botsford School of Dance in Rochester, New York. As the director he hopes to accomplish in Rochester some of the goals he realized at ABT, such as a wide range of graded instruction and classes, and admission for aspiring critics and directors, to say nothing of a rounded education in all facets of ballet history, performance, and production.

His regrets no longer even linger. From the moment when he was a 13-year-old supernumerary watching Alexandra Danilova from the wings and deciding to be a dancer, to the agonizing day when his performing career ended, Danielian has always looked forward with intense desire to bringing along a new generation of dancers.

He has a lot to give, and it is a hallmark that great teachers must fulfill their destinies—not to coin a cliché—or perish within. As with most master teachers, Danielian's professional background, on which his present eminence is based, is impeccable. He was the first winner of *Dance Magazine*'s Dancer of The Year Award. He possesses the Dance Teaching Award of Dance Masters of America, and he has been decorated five times by heads of state.

Almost his entire dance education was acquired under Mordkin, and it was with the Mordkin Ballet in 1937 that he made his professional debut in the Peasant Pas de Deux from *Giselle*. He danced with Mordkin for two years, then joined the new Ballet Theatre in 1939 (long before the American Ballet Theatre came into being) and stayed two years there. The period was interspersed with work in night clubs and on Broadway as a means of furthering his career and helping to support his family. Among the shows were *Song of Norway* and *I Married An Angel,* in which George Balanchine was the choreographer and Danielian a member of the chorus.

He joined Ballets Russes de Monte Carlo in 1943 at the age of 23 and stayed through 1958, when pain forced him into guest artist roles. And he retired from dancing in 1959.

He also appeared with the San Francisco Ballet, Boris Kochno's Ballet des Champs Élysées, and the Louisville (Kentucky) Civic Ballet among many such groups. He partnered some of the greatest ballerinas of the day, among them the two Alicias, Alonso and Markova, Maria Tallchief, and Danilova, and danced in much of the current repertoire. Roles closely associated with him were in *Afternoon of a Faun, Le Beau Danube, Danses Concertantes, Frankie and Johnny, Gaité Parisienne, Mozartiana, Serenade, Sheherazade, Snow Maiden,* and *Les Sylphides.*

Danielian did not, fortunately, suffer the withdrawal symptoms many dancers do when they leave the stage. He became a teacher because he wanted to, and the profession thus enfolded an unembittered man. Resigned though he may have been, Danielian's turmoils did not interfere with his plans for something like the complete ballet school the Russian system used to run.

Thus, although American Ballet Theatre School students may remain unindoctrinated in higher mathematics and ancient history they are launched into a system of orderly instruction that, when given the opportunity, will carry them footsure from first position to final glory.

Danielian immediately set the tone with the drama of his teaching, the pride and dignity of his classroom example. If his students depart from a lesson with nothing more substantial in their skulls than that, they do leave with a sense of having touched splendor. Danielian has shown them pride in their profession and, what is more evanescent, pride in themselves. If they can hold onto that until the next lesson they will be halfway to wonder.

Danielian minimizes his contribution. "I really don't teach. I like to think that I open doors, as an analyst does, perhaps, and show them the knowledge of what technique is about, so that when they look in a mirror they will know what correct placement of the body should be, what the correct terminology is—things like that. I want them to understand how like sculptors they are and that their bodies are lumps of clay to be molded. I don't do the molding; they do."

Perhaps not now any longer, since Danielian's increasing administrative duties leave little time for teaching, but the teaching he does do, and his philosophies, are a distillate of those fine juices from all the years. He believes that ideally ballet dancers should be trained to dance anything, and that it is not always in their best interests to be prepared in a single style or accustomed to a single brand of choreography. The horizons are limited enough, he says.

He aches for smaller classes, more teachers cast in a certain mold, and more leisure to inculcate the young in the value of the other arts as related to dancing—and more leisure for them to visit museums and galleries, and attend concerts, and explore literature and history—the complete school, in other words.

But that era died with Diaghilev, and there is barely time now even to suggest. American Ballet Theatre School is too large (900 students during the course of a year) for much individual attention, except minimally. And besides, students these days wander from one school to another, from one style to another, from one teacher to another, so that it is impossible to bring the bud to bloom without interruption.

Still, teachers such as Danielian are constantly consulted. On occasion other teachers dispatch promising students for his magic touch or all-seeing eye, and established dancers come to him for coaching.

As for class, the day is too short, would-be dancers too many, and teachers too few to spend time fruitlessly on youngsters unprepared to invest their all. "I was brought up to believe that if someone really wanted to dance, you must do everything for them. And I try to. But if there is someone who looks the other way, as it were, who is inattentive, who isn't ready for the give-and-take of class—or, indeed, who may not even know what give-and-take is about—then I ask that person to leave.

"I like to look at a class, for the first time or the tenth time it doesn't matter, and have them stand at attention, and right then and there it is possible to know how far one can go. You can see whether they are there to work—the lift of the chest, the slump of the shoulder, the character of the head—and, within an hour I know where I'm at. I don't care if the students are fat or untalented or what, but if they really, sincerely, from the depths want to dance, we'll find a place for them."

Since nearly all teachers, and certainly the great ones, were dancers at one time, they need, Danielian says, to overcome their own problems before beginning to attack those of the class. The major one is how not to deliver instruction in the style to which they were accustomed, but to close the curtain finally on their own performing careers while helping students raise the curtain on theirs.

Another problem is to understand the imperishable value of ABCs—

creating the "basic body," the line and placement which are to style what crawling is to walking, "so that dancers will look beautiful no matter what they do. Style develops later, much later from the gut and soul of the dancer, and that is no longer a matter for the classroom, but for coaching."

Danielian likens the wall-to-wall mirror of the classroom to a proscenium curtain in the theater that has lifted to expose the student to a wonderland audience where both his best and his not-so-good are on instant replay. At once, one is struck by the hallmarks of a Danielian product—pride and dignity, chest out, head drawn back and up, face faintly wreathed in self-esteem—with the corner of an eye aimed at the reflection in the glass.

It is no less than the example of their urbane and courtly mentor—the father figure in the mirror, dramatic and proud, assuming without effort "Basic Body Posture No. 1," the unbroken line from toe to top trailing off in a wisp of panache.

And so Danielian strolls eagle-eyed about the studio, in and out among his students, managing affairs almost by vocal timbre alone, gesticulating, snapping fingers, clapping hands, rolling his R's, singing along, conferring moments of instruction at the barre, and beating an inexorable time.

As with all master teachers this is a virtuoso performance, unpracticed, unforced, delicious to watch. And as with all the great ones, Danielian cares and shows it. Always, in a corner of his eye, there is a lurking concern, an ocular wringing of hands. Now and then, though, the pieces fall into place, and the benediction of his wide grin is worth waiting for. A generation of students thinks so.

Felia Doubrovska

Left: An early photo of Felia Doubrovska, taken in Russia, shows the dancer in a costume designed by Leon Bakst for "Lezhginka," a folk dance used by Glinka in his opera, *A Life for the Tsar.*

Below left: Doubrovska as the Hostess in Bronislava Nijinska's ballet, *Les Biches,* as she appeared at the premiere performance with the Diaghilev Ballets Russes in the Théâtre de Monte Carlo, Jan. 6, 1924.

Below: Pierre Vladimiroff, circa 1920.

Above: Doubrovska partnered by Serge Lifar in a pose from *Les Sylphides* (1926) when both were members of the Diaghilev Ballets Russes. The setting is out-of-doors.

Left: Pavlova near the end of her life, and Doubrovska in Monte Carlo, 1930.

Left: Teaching at the School of American Ballet. September, 1958. Photo by Martha Swope.

Below left: In a class in Cologne, 1963. Photo by Hubert Simon.

Below: Doubrovska in her apartment, 1976, still tall, shapely and regal. Photo by Klaus Aufdembrinke.

Right: Ever graceful, Doubrovska instructs mixed class at the School of American Ballet, 1958. Photo by Martha Swope.

I T IS A CLICHÉ, one supposes, to refer to people as national treasures—and the man in the street or in the balcony might legitimately wonder, "Felia who?"

But Felia Doubrovska in her eighth decade becomes more cherishable by the hour. She is one of the few remaining links with the golden past. She danced for Diaghilev and knew Karsavina, Pavlova, Nijinsky, and everyone else. Her spare, upright frame is a chalice filled with the purity of mission—to tell it how it was . . . in the School of the Imperial Russian Ballet . . . in the old Maryinsky Theater . . . to the inheritors of Petipa . . . transmitting sacred forms in the manner in which they were conceived . . . helping to mold a generation of dancers according to the gospel of the old, and true, Russian ballet.

Doubrovska was a serious dancer and is equally serious as a teacher. She is artistically and constitutionally unable to spend her time on students whose goal is, for instance, to lose weight. The art of ballet, to her, has always been a higher calling, and though she may not herself use the phrase she is indeed a torchbearer whose flame burns brightly at the School of American Ballet, affiliate of the New York City Ballet.

Born Felizata Dloujnevska in St. Petersburg, Doubrovska was enrolled in the School of the Imperial Russian Ballet at the age of 10 with reluctant parental consent after friends advised that ballet training would cure her fragility. It did, and she was graduated at the age of 17 with her present name—which, as long as she was going to pursue a professional career, was selected as easier to pronounce.

Doubrovska and Olga Spessivtseva were graduated at the same time at the top of their class, and accordingly were given the honor of wearing white dresses at their graduation and of selecting their own *pas de deux* to perform.

Doubrovska fled the country in 1920 on skis, but before that and following her graduation she was a member of the Imperial Russian Ballet, first in the corps and then in larger roles—physically as well as artistically. At a regal 5 feet 6 inches tall she danced the Big Swan in *Swan Lake.*

"Here you don't have this part. Here you dance small swans. I was Big Swan. Another Big Swan was the mother of Galina Ulanova."

It was a fashion for families with means to summer away from the cities—in the Russian countryside or abroad. Doubrovska remembers that her parents rented a cottage in Finland in 1913. There, summer after summer, they became friendly with the man destined to save perhaps their lives and certainly Doubrovska's career.

As the years passed and family members died, Doubrovska and her mother, Valentina, their perimeters shrunken, lived the year around in St. Petersburg with very little of anything to their names during World War I and the Russian Revolution.

On one of the darker days their friend from Finland turned up with gifts of bread and butter, and asked whether they would like to leave Russia. "He brought some other people who wanted to leave, and he said maybe we would all like to go. Everything had been confiscated. All we had was hope. The banks were closed; our savings were gone.

"My mother said, 'Yes!' and he said 'You have to decide now, today, this minute, because now we can go by skis as if we are enjoying ourselves. No one will notice. Later on the snow will be soft and it will take more time, and there are too many risks.' Well, I was rehearsing at the Maryinsky, and when I came home my mother said 'We are going!' We took nothing with us. We left right away, that day."

Doubrovska remembers that about a dozen others were in the party, among them Pierre Vladimiroff, who was to become famous as a dancer and teacher, and was later Doubrovska's husband. The savior from Finland led his straggling party to within a mile of the Finnish border, pointed out the way, and advised them that they were on their own. Doubrovska and friends made it safely into Finland. They were placed in quarantine for a month with the warning that they must be prepared to emigrate after that time or be returned to Russia.

Vladimiroff, who had been graduated three years before Doubrovska and already had danced two seasons with the Diaghilev Ballets Russes, one time as a replacement for Nijinsky, wrote to Diaghilev in Paris. The impresario happened to be in Spain at the time and did not receive the message.

Doubrovska's mother had better luck. In a reply from Maria Kouznetsova, a Russian friend who was singing with the Paris Opera, Mme. Doubrovska learned there were two weeks before the annual Grand Prix race (after which everybody who was anybody departed on holiday) to arrange for a dance recital. Kouznetsova sent money and necessary documents, and mother, daughter, and husband-to-be reached safety in France.

The concert went off splendidly in the grand Théâtre des Champs-Elysées. Doubrovska danced to Riccardo Drigo's *Valse Bluette*. Diaghilev engaged the couple on the basis of the glowing reviews, and they entered the company the following season. Although Vladimiroff was destined to have the larger career, Doubrovska's long, expressive legs and supple spine were sufficient to inspire George Balanchine to create for her the role of the Siren in *The Prodigal Son*. She was also the first to dance the Bride in Bronislava Nijinska's *Les Noces*. Elegance and aristocratic grace were Doubrovska's mantle, and her incomparable feet with their flexible, high-arched insteps helped establish her reputation. She has lost none of these attributes.

Events proceeded swiftly; Doubrovska and Vladimiroff were married in England in January, 1921. Although Doubrovska remained with the Ballets Russes until Diaghilev's death in 1929, Vladimiroff accepted an offer to tour with Tamara Karsavina from 1924 to 1927 and with the company of Anna Pavlova from 1927 until her death in 1931. With Karsavina he visited the United States for the first time in 1924.

The demands of the Vladimiroffs' individual careers kept them apart for long periods of time. When Vladimiroff was on tour, which was for months on end, Doubrovska and the Ballets Russes generally swung around a European orbit. The couple maintained an apartment in Paris where Mme. Doubrovska kept the home fires burning and to which the two dancers gravitated whenever they could be together. After Diaghilev's death and the dissolution of his company Doubrovska joined her husband under Pavlova's banner for the final year of the company during Pavlova's lifetime.

Shortly, Vladimiroff yielded to the persuasion of George Balanchine to come to the United States under the sponsorship of Lincoln Kirstein and teach at the School of American Ballet, which Balanchine was to found in 1934. It was Balanchine's desire to transfer the Russian tradition to modern shores, and this also figured in his reason for later engaging Doubrovska.

At any rate, Doubrovska stayed in Paris when Vladimiroff went to New York, and each visited the other on all possible occasions. Meanwhile, Doubrovska danced for two years with a company organized by Serge Lifar and one season after that as a guest artist at the Teatro Colon in Buenos Aires at the invitation of Dimitri Romanoff, then ballet master there, today regisseur of American Ballet Theatre.

Vladimiroff was in France on vacation in 1940 when the darkling skies over Europe so alarmed their American friends that a cablegram from the States implored the couple to leave while they could. Through the intervention of René Blum, founder of the Ballets Russes de Monte Carlo, Colonel Vassili de Basil, the director, offered Doubrovska a place with the company. Vladimiroff needed no position, since he already was employed at the School of American Ballet.

"When the offer came, mama and Pierre ran all the way to the theater where I was, to tell me, they were so happy."

De Basil's offer was a device to permit Doubrovska to leave France. She and Vladimiroff went directly to Amsterdam and from there to the United States, where they bought a house in Lakewood, New Jersey. Vladimiroff resumed teaching. Doubrovska enjoyed friends, theaters, reading, parties until she accepted an offer in 1945 to perform as ballerina with the Metropolitan Opera Ballet. She declined to renew her contract the following year, wishing to spend more time with mama. Mme. Doubrovska died in 1947, and a year later Doubrovska joined her husband as a teacher in the School of American Ballet. Except for a heart attack in 1976, and a stroke three years later, Doubrovska has taught at the school ever since.

On several occasions she tried to retire, but always Balanchine expressed his continuing need of her, and she acquiesced. She admits that retirement might not provide the most salubrious climate for the remaining years of her life, yet she is deeply wounded by the heedless manners in the modern nimbus of her days.

She is severely conscious that there is no instructor at the school older than she, that her contemporaries are vanishing, that others seldom wish to be bothered even with amenities.

"Yesterday they [her students] take my class; today they don't recognize me. I don't think they really need me. They admire influence, and they want people who are important. I never ask anyone for anything, and I don't want to be pitied. When I die, everything will go. Perhaps it is best to close now and go to a rest home—to read, to live in the past."

This is spoken with the heart flung open, and it is a cry from another age. Doubrovska has been alone since her husband died in 1971—alone except for Lala, the Yorkshire terrier who owns her—and each of her days now is a victory. She survives because her pride permits nothing else. But behind closed doors there is anguish.

Yet she is never less than gracious, never less than charming, and she walks perpetually in an aura of mauve and memory. It is this remembrance of things past that she conveys to her students, for the manner is partly the message. And the way things used to be—the lexicon of the Russian school—is still hard and vital. Doubrovska studied, after all, with Pavel Gerdt, Christian Johansson, and Enrico Cecchetti, and her knowledge is to be received with gravity and worship.

Some of it rubs off, and it is rather marvelous to watch her in class. Her figure is good enough still to be displayed in leotards, and when she illustrates, there is a star quality in that patrician form.

She moves in adagio, instructs in a muted voice, and misses nothing. "I look in the mirror. I see everything. I see what you do. So, behave!" She teaches the way she herself was taught. It is not only Petipa and Maryinsky. What she gives her girls (she no longer teaches mixed classes) in *attitudes* and *arabesques en face* is the way they were executed in a day when technique was not the answer to everything.

Dancers are stronger today, in her view, but artistry in general is not. When she was a dancer, the 32 fouettes were a feat. Today it does not take much to do them. But on the other side, dancers once infused their roles with tempest and fire and magic. Today, expressionism might be considered old-fashioned, like silent movies. Yet, is bloodlessness more desirable?

"Today, when I come to class, I come with good wish, not just to say what is wrong. I know that when somebody is not correct in class I don't say something rude, but very nicely I correct them and approach every girl differently."

What they do at the barre is as important as what they do in the center, and later in center stage, she says, because even warmup movement should spring from the soul, just as if the curtain were up.

Doubrovska's credo is humanistic; all else is assumed. "My pupils must, first of all, be dedicated to ballet, and love it—not do anything mechanically, but feel and know every movement, its reason, what it expresses. They must become the part they are dancing.

"Every pupil needs individual study. I have to be able to recognize what she feels, notice symptoms of insecurity, find out if there are physical, personal, or emotional reasons that would make her work difficult, and help her to overcome them without making it obvious.

"One of my principles is not to work pupils too hard, so that even if they are tired after a lesson they would still be perfectly at ease and eager to continue after a short rest. I really feel as if I were inside a pupil, as if I were she, and I know whether she tried too hard or just pretends. I try to teach with understanding, remembering from my own experience how a harsh word can so easily affect the desire to work. When I have a large class and need to make a general remark I always try to look at every girl separately so that each feels noticed, even if only by a meeting of our eyes.

"The teacher herself must love what she is doing. Even when no longer a dancer herself, she should feel that, in giving her pupils the steps and movements, she is actually dancing them herself. A good teacher should explain the reason for every movement, since many of them form the foundation upon which most ballets are built. I also believe greatly in discipline. If I have to repeat the same correction or comment for several sessions to one girl, I then ignore her for the next class or two. I well know this is felt keenly and almost always brings desired results. This discipline covers every detail connected with the class, such as being on time, being properly dressed, with slippers and dress in perfect condition, and so forth."

Doubrovska demands coordination, harmony, and control. It makes for both discipline and clarity of mind, she says. "Not only discipline in class, but self-discipline. That, and instilling confidence, is one of the teacher's first tasks.

"Ballet is a delicate art, but it requires more will power and self-discipline than any other art. It expresses the strongest feelings of a human being— from the deepest despair and anger to the purest and most ecstatic joy."

On days when she is teaching, attired for class with a wisp of skirt about her waist, Doubrovska tiptoes through the corridors of the School of American Ballet, Lala cuddled in her arms, carefully sidestepping all the brasher types—which is everyone—until she is inside her studio. Then, with Lala, an old ballet hand, safely deposited, she steps into the center to begin. The girls are hushed, and the next 1½ hours are spent in a cathedral. Yes, there is the rehearsal piano; yes, Madame speaks and instructs; yes, visitors slip respectfully in and out. But despite the susurrus of extraneous sound Doubrovska's class is more of a temple than any other studio in the place, and by coincidence her girls are dressed in white.

Left: The simmering passion evident in Valentina Pereyaslavec's teaching also is evident in this 1941 portrait of the artist as a prima ballerina of the Opera Ballet in Lvov.

Below: Surrounded by admirers, Pereyaslavec returns the amenities of Rudolf Nureyev and Erik Bruhn, with Margot Fonteyn and Carla Fracci smiling their approval. Photo by Martha Swope.

Above: In one of many open classes conducted by Pereyaslavec in the 1960s, to which members of foreign companies, then in the United States, flocked, she is here instructing Derek Rencher of The Royal Ballet; Carla Fracci of American Ballet Theatre; Maria Tallchief of New York City Ballet, fourth from left, and Rudolf Nureyev, then with The Royal Ballet, last on left. Other two dancers are unidentified. Photo by Martha Swope.

Left: Warming up at the old Metropolitan Opera House prior to a performance, Rudolf Nureyev takes his cues from Madame. About 1964. Photo by Richard Avedon.

Left: Although Madame wears her hair differently from the style in this 1968 photograph, the facial features are essentially unchanged. Photo by Roy Round.

Below: At one time Loyce Houlton, artistic director of the Minnesota Dance Theater and School, brought an entire class to New York City to take instruction from Pereyaslavec at the former quarters of the American Ballet Theatre School. Photo by Myron Papiz.

Right: At a national conference and seminar of the Cecchetti Council of America, at Michigan State University, East Lansing, Pereyaslavec works her magic upon a cadre of young hopefuls on the floor of a gymnasium. Photo courtesy of Michigan State University.

WHEN VALENTINA PEREYASLAVEC emigrated to the United States and turned to teaching ballet, the army lost a fine drill sergeant.

In the sense that she can be likened to no one on her level, Pereyaslavec is incomparable. She is a true original, flamboyant, spirited, stentorian, feisty, and with the proverbial heart of gold. The voice may shake the rafters, but the gleaming eyes are soft. At the American Ballet Theatre School where she teaches she is affectionately known as Madame Perry. There is evidence that she dislikes the shortened name, and when she vocalizes displeasure her words speed like daggers hurled at the heart or the jugular. No one knowingly excites her ire, for she is a great attacker.

All this is not to suggest that Pereyaslavec is an ogress. She is a love, actually, and is widely sought by young students for the benefit of her uncompromising views on excellence.

A recent visitor to her class recorded the following impressions, and they are a graphic indicator of Pereyaslavec the teacher:

"She is in absolute charge. There is no doubt or equivocation when she issues an instruction. She spins out combinations verbally in French and visually in front of the mirror so that her students can record the image and she can see them. She strings out her combinations. They're fairly long, and the kids remember them. She stamps her feet a lot and snaps her fingers. She has a fingersnap like a whip. She doesn't waste a moment. Her classes are lean. She demands instant obedience and always says 'Thank you!' She moves her people about like markers, directing who gets into what line, and where. She is a passionate teacher moved as much by the melodies from her piano as by the demands of her art. She emphasizes balance and legato. Her hair is drawn up in a very tight bun— more tightly than those of her girls.

"When all five feet of her get angry, watch out. She isn't putting on a show. She is angry not only because there are mistakes, but because ballet has been violated. She teaches by example. When she says 'You do this!' or 'You don't do this!' it holds for all time. She is ramrod straight, head high, chin up. The girls can wear rings and earrings and wrist watches, but she doesn't like it. She forbids anyone talking in class but herself. At the end, not only do they applaud, but they shout 'Bravo! Bravo!' "

The fiery, or sparkling, Pereyaslavec (depending upon who, what, when, where, and why) could not have been destined for anything less than success. She had a fine career as a prima ballerina in Russia when World War II came along and tore her life apart. The hiatus from performing, incarceration in a Ukrainian displaced persons camp, and privation on all levels effectively ended her days as a major dancer. In the dislocation that followed liberation, Pereyaslavec plowed through doubts, uncertainties, and rumors about the advantages and hazards of resettlement and took the only course open to her—due west.

She took with her the training, discipline, and tradition of the Soviet Choreographic Technicum (now the Bolshoi Ballet School) and the Kirov State Ballet School, to say nothing of the experiences at the Kharkov Opera-Ballet Theater, where she was one of three prima ballerinas, and the city of Lvov, where she also was a prima. Then, war. After liberation she danced for American soldiers and displaced persons under the aegis of the United Nations Relief and Rehabilitation Agency, and she established an *école de danse* in the detention camp which was her residence. She was able to save $11 to take her to America—where, she once told an interviewer, she arrived with a winter coat made from a German army blanket, a coffee pot, and two left shoes because they were the only ones she could find.

Pereyaslavec was as brave as any and luckier than most, for there was a Ukrainian Relief Committee to meet her in Philadelphia and allay her fears. But she began on her own, immediately, to seek employment under the severe handicap of language. There were the inevitable refusals and finally the first job—cleaning peaches in a food processing plant. Later she became a packer in a cigar factory.

She made small mention of her history in ballet simply because no one expressed inordinate interest, not even schools where she offered her services in the evening without charge.

Though alone in some respects, Pereyaslavec was not alone in others. In the warm, tightly knit Ukrainian community of Philadelphia and New York many were familiar with her background and career—and word traveled. It was, after all, unseemly for a ballerina to be packing cigars ("Like Carmen, you know . . .").

After four months of odoriferous labor Pereyaslavec opened a letter one day from her former accompanist on the UNRRA tours who suggested that there might be a teaching position in the New York studio of Tatyana Semyonova at Carnegie Hall. One Saturday morning she went there and was asked, with apologies, to audition, since that was the way in America. Moments later Semyonova stopped her and offered a three-year contract.

Pereyaslavec worked one more week at the cigar factory, and when her employer asked with wonder whether she was truly a prima ballerina, Pereyaslavec replied "Oh, no, I am just amateur dancer, and I want to go back to my profession." Her co-workers, who were not in the know, and her Ukrainian friends, who were, gave her a farewell party whose memory still leaves her flushed with pleasure.

It did not take long for news of this brilliant new teacher to waft down the block to Ballet Theatre, where members of the company came to see, were conquered, and stayed. Among them were Eric Braun, Scott Douglas, Nora Kaye, Ruth Ann Koesun, John Kriza, Barbara Lloyd, Paula Lloyd, Norma Vance, and Jenny Workman—all of whom began to take class with Pereyaslavec whenever possible. Soon Lucia Chase, founder and director of Ballet Theatre, invited the pint-sized firebrand to join her staff. A year later, in 1951, she did.

"This is happiest day of my life. This is when my life in United States begin," she says. Pereyaslavec has been teaching at the American Ballet Theatre School ever since. With her is her alter ego, Valentina Vishnevskaya ("My Valya")—with whom conversation and instruction are needless—at the piano. The partnership is one of two bodies and a single mind. Dame Marie Rambert once remarked: "You and Valya work in such unison, it is like a symphony. How she understands you and senses your every requirement!"

Pereyaslavec's studio soon included, among others, Eleanor D'Antuono, Sonia Arova, Svetlana Beriosova, Oleg Briansky, Erik Bruhn,

William Carter, Royes Fernandez, Carla Fracci, Tatiana Grantzeva, Melissa Hayden, Rosella Hightower, Ivan Nagy, Lupe Serrano, Maria Tallchief, Marjorie Tallchief, and Violette Verdy.

She helped train Rudolf Nureyev, who loves her and brought Margot Fonteyn into the fold. The passion according to Pereyaslavec draws acolytes from all the visiting ballet companies, to say nothing of Broadway and nightclubs.

"If you can survive Madame's barre, you can survive anything," Fonteyn was quoted as saying. Never one for understatement, Verdy wrote on the occasion of Pereyaslavec's 25th anniversary at American Ballet Theatre: "The power Mme. Pereyaslavec exercises over the students: an intense, stoic discipline, rewarded by exploding into a vibrant sense of rhythm, creating an almost heroic exaltation." Brian Shaw of The Royal Ballet called her unequivocally "one of the most wonderful teachers in the western world." William Carter said: "From her unending reservoir of talent, energy and imagination she makes each class fresh, vital and unforgettable. She enters the studio like a shaft of sunlight."*

These and all other accolades and tributes are filled as much with love as with appreciation—and the respect is monumental. Anyone whose brief sojourn brushes hers recognizes Pereyaslavec's total commitment to dance.

She does nothing by halves, or even quarters, and she gives no quarter in the classroom. As with all reputable teachers she is solely committed to excellence and soulfully pursues it. The perfection she seeks to instill in others comes from within them, she says, "from the soul," and is exposed and burnished simply by work, work, and more work. There is no substitute, and all other considerations being equal, practice indeed makes perfect, according to Pereyaslavec. It has, so often as to lend credence to her creed.

Our time is no longer an age of the pioneer. All the principles have been discovered, at least in ballet it would seem, and most teachers today pick and choose from the lexicons of yesterday's great teachers in the formulation of what in architecture is called the international style. Today's teaching is governed more by the demands of modern choreography than by the lessons of the past. Thus Pereyaslavec is no one's disciple, though if she hews to anyone it is probably to Agrippina Vaganova, the great Russian teacher who seldom discarded a duckling because it was not a swan.

Pereyaslavec's view is that there is no possibility unworthy of probability, and no probability that cannot be coaxed or bullied, as the case may be, into certainty. She is her own best example. As a prima ballerina in Kharkov, winning ecstatic reviews, she first saw visiting dancers from

Leningrad perform and was appalled at what she perceived to be her own shortcomings by comparision. She began to work all over again. Later, when her company performed in Leningrad, high praise notwithstanding, her personal dissatisfaction dictated that she must take a different road. She ended her career temporarily to restudy the basics at Leningrad's Choreographic Technicum, and was not above watching and working from the last row of the corps until satisfied that her *épaulement* was now correct and her faults erased. After three years of this she took the stage again as the prima ballerina of a company in Lvov. It was the eve of World War II, and although the applause has not ended yet, Pereyaslavec's career as a dancer was nearly over.

There are no regrets. Pereyaslavec has the rare facility of drawing light from darkness. She is a positive thinker, and what was yesterday, was yesterday. One is not at all certain that she might not like to take a trip on a time machine, but so long as she is ensorceled in the present dimension she extracts from it every ounce of living.

Her flame burns most brightly, of course, in her work. A feature of her classes is the instant choreography of her combinations. She spins them out like silk, a coruscating series of steps like 60-second ballets sprung without repetition from her imagination to illustrate a dozen points at once. In such times as these she faces the class like an orchestra conductor, the baton of her presence uplifted only to crash down on: "*And!* . . ." the eternal signal to the piano. And the sweating students embark grimly on ten, twelve, fourteen instructions that flow from the memory imbedded in her muscles.

Her classes are unplanned. "I am teacher too long to prepare night before. No need. I am ballerina and teacher together from earliest time." In classes she took with Asaf Messerer at the Bolshoi Ballet School years ago, Messerer would occasionally leave the studio, she says, and invariably would turn the class over to her. "Maybe I have talent teaching, and Messerer know that. So, I give adagio."

Every martinet has foibles, and Pereyaslavec is no exception. She cannot abide students who have the temerity to tell her they cannot abide working next to someone they do not like. Work and concentration are all, she devoutly believes, and personalities must not be allowed to interfere. Yet her own fierce concentration can be thrown askew by something so seemingly insignificant as a spot of color. In one of her classes one day she was thrown off by a girl's red practice clothes. No, she has nothing against red, but not that red. "Same as bull. I no like."

Pereyaslavec's cultural interests are broad. In earlier years she was a frequent habitué of the opera house, concert hall, Broadway shows, and the movies. "But now I go mostly to matinees, because I afraid to go at night. Sometimes I have free tickets, and I look at the boys and girls who come here and not have money to go to theater, and I invite them to come with me."

What does that do to the student-teacher relationship? "No relationship. Only ice cream. You know, in class I am psychologist, nana, mama, doctor, everything. In class, we . . . enemy. Outside class I am always friend."

*Quotations from *Dance News,* December, 1976.

Left: Karel Shook as the Baron in George Balanchine's *La Sonnambula,* in Amsterdam (circa 1967). Except for the bone structure, small resemblance to the Karel Shook of today, even discounting the makeup.

Below left: In the studio. Arthur Mitchell, founder and director of the Dance Theatre of Harlem, with his co-director. Photo by Marbeth.

Below: Karel Shook in a characteristic moment of conversation.

Right: With (from left) Louis Johnson, Sadie Feddoes, Arthur Mitchell, Cicely Tyson, Dionne Warwicke and Brock Peters.

Below right: At the DTH, observing a class, are Princess Margaret and Lord Snowdon, with Judy and Samuel Peabody in the back row, and Shook, lost in thought, at right. Photo by Marbeth.

Left: Shook, in class at the Dance Theatre of Harlem.

Below left: In class at the Dance Theatre of Harlem, the blackboard pointer in evidence. Shook uses the pointer like a baton and a pointer, but rarely touches dancers with it.

Below: Karel Shook is said by many to be a superior cook. His food processor helps.

Right: Behind barres. Shook relaxes at one and watches, missing nothing.

Photos by Marbeth.

KAREL SHOOK, co-director (with Arthur Mitchell) of the Dance Theatre of Harlem, practices what most other teachers merely preach.

No instructor can be all bad who says: "The dance teacher must be involved with the total human being, because the dancer's body is an instrument which eventually has to be able to reflect all states of the psyche. . . . The emotions have to be controlled if objectivity, which is a prerequisite of good teaching and good learning, is to be preserved. . . . The teacher's function is to transmit knowledge and not display it on the lapel like a decoration. . . ."*

Shook cares, really cares, and although he is scarcely a champion talker his written words convey a wide range of understanding and the depth of his concern for the individual whom he prizes for qualities that are unique in everyone. He is to other teachers what medical specialists are to general practitioners, and the fact that he felt impelled to write a manual of instruction in a day when such things are nearly out of style says something about his profound knowledge of dance and the posthypnotic urge to tell what he knows. How many new things, after all, are being said about dance instruction these days? How many pathfinders are left?

All of what Shook says in his slender volume is of course known, tacitly or not, but his exercises are useful and there is always the unspoken assurance that wherever he is the written words of history are in motion. Thus within the walls of the Dance Theatre of Harlem, which is something of a university (or at least a junior college) of the theater, Karel Shook, an acknowledged master, is administering a tradition descended from father to son, from pupil to pupil, and so shall be for immemorial time.

Shook is not so much an avatar of the golden age as an exemplar of its basic training. Despite a cool and rather impersonal manner he is passionately interested in ages 8 to 13, the years when most dancers are made, and there is a finger-shaking sternness overlaid with restrained parental love about his way of expressing himself in the studio.

An *eminence grise,* as one student referred to him, Shook conducts a class or rehearsal in the lowest of keys, fading in and out of sight like a wraith, never raising his voice, and missing nothing. "The body never lies," he says, echoing Martha Graham. "People reveal themselves, what they are thinking, how they think, how fast they think, how long they can concentrate, how much stamina and strength and physical weaknesses they have." An erring body draws Shook like a homing pigeon, and in seconds he is at the body's side, counseling and fixing, lifting an arm here, pushing a head to one side there, stretching a finger, propping up a leg. But gently, always gently. "You see, art emanates from humanity, and we are dealing first with human beings and secondly with dancers."

One has the impression that Shook chafes under the burden of appreciation. He discourages applause for the teacher at the end of a lesson and, similarly, starts lessons without even a grace note. "O.K., people, let's face the barre" (in his grey, noncommittal voice), and work begins. Sometimes a cigarette droops from his lips; sometimes he carries a blackboard pointer—for pointing, not for touching. He roams the studio telegraphing instructions calmly, simply, seriously in a voice which for Shook seems less than other people's voices—but they hear him, even above the piano. One wonders how they are able to, yet that is part of the discipline. Many teachers use the same technique.

He conducts a "hard" class, in the sense of small surcease. From time to time he will say, "Take a breath." One breath later, class resumes. There is no time for more. Students are paying good money to try and achieve something money cannot buy, and Shook feels bound by honor to establish the one-to-one relationship that will permit the student to identify, each for himself, what dancing is all about.

It is not about dancing as such. "What the dancer does physically," Shook says, "is not of maximum importance. It is how the dancer enlivens the space in which he moves that is important. This is the concept that must be learned."

There is no better mentor than Shook, who understands how vital it is to develop "an objectively controlled intimacy between teacher and student—complete truthfulness and honesty, a naked human response, trust, communication." The teacher's capability in this area is a born gift, Shook believes. It doesn't just happen, and it cannot be acquired—at least to one's optimum satisfaction and especially with children.

"You have to look children straight in the eyes. If you don't you're in trouble. They don't trust you. Kids are canny. If you speak abstractly, they don't get it. Children are much more aware than adults, because they don't have the overlay of experience."

Thus it is especially and vitally important that teachers of the young know what they are about. One should mention that Shook takes a dim view of teachers in general, and probably with cause. He has seen too much to remain unaffected by sophistry in the profession he seeks to elevate.

Disaffection scarcely disguised, Shook writes: "Too many teachers concern themselves solely with a pragmatic routine that they are convinced cannot fail provided they follow the rules." And he verbalizes: "The teacher who does not have an acutely developed sense of communication, and the inner need to transmit, is the instrument of routine. As a student you may do arbitrarily what you are told to do, but that is not good teaching, because the boys and girls are not learning, except by rote.

"The dancer is, or should be, involved emotionally, physically, mentally and spiritually. The whole thing has to come together, and although this may sound a bit mystic, it really isn't. Emotion and spirit should be fostered first—the way dancers manage their inner feelings and approach to particular movement, rather than their execution of that movement. You just don't do an arabesque. You become the arabesque.

"Too much dance teaching is involved with posing. You go from one pose to another pose to another pose, and there are no transitions, no breaths. Another big fault is that many teachers teach a phrase of movement, movement by movement. In other words, it is as if I were to teach a poem word-for-word rather than a paragraph at a time or the whole idea or whole thought."

The exponent of this and similar items of wisdom is native to Renton, Washington, where at the age of 13 he set out to become an actor. Three years later he won a statewide contest with a reading of Aase's Death from Ibsen's *Peer Gynt,* on the surface an inappropriate choice for a growing boy, but one which today symbolizes Shook's seriousness superbly.

By all accounts Shook was unusually talented. Soon he started to study dance, which displaced acting as his primary interest and brought him at the age of 19 to the attention of Leonide Massine. There followed an invitation from Massine to join the Ballets Russes de Monte Carlo, which one suspects the upwardly mobile Shook accepted without urging. He made his debut with that company in November 1939 at the Metropolitan Opera House in New York City, as the Beggar in Massine's *St. Francis* (Noblissima Visione), which Shook considered a favorable omen since his middle name is Francis.

Shook was to leave the company and join it again twice during the formative periods of his career. In the times between, he "retired" in order to resume studying dance; he acted, danced, and assisted on the technical side with a touring show called *Doodle Dandy*; he toured with the national companies of *The Chocolate Soldier* and *Song of Norway*; and he danced for a season with the New York City Ballet.

Finally, in 1950, he returned to the Ballets Russes de Monte Carlo for the last time as a dancer, mime, and assistant ballet master, and he began seriously to teach. Two years later, at the age of 32, his metier surfaced at last, and he joined the Katherine Dunham School as head of the ballet department. Among his students were Arthur Mitchell, Geoffrey Holder, and Alvin Ailey, who continued their studies and at the same time taught classes as faculty in Shook's own school, Studio of Dance Arts, which he opened after the Dunham School closed in 1954.

Other dancers flocked to study with him, among them Mary Hinkson, Matt Turney, and Robert Cohan from the Martha Graham company, and Shook began to choreograph. His first ballet, a pas de deux called *Souvenir* for Alexandra Danilova and Michael Lland, was well received.

In 1957 Shook closed up shop and joined the faculty of the June Taylor School. Two years later he accepted the position of ballet master and first teacher at the then Netherlands Ballet. During the nine years of his tenure in Holland his name and fame surmounted the barriers to the ballet world and became familiar to everwidening circles of people interested in the arts.

This may have been due in part to the mime repertoire he was persuaded to take on with the Dutch troupe. But more important were the more than twenty works he choreographed for stage, opera, and television on both sides of the Atlantic; acting as technical adviser and a director of dances for television; teaching elsewhere in Europe; writing about dance in numerous articles for newspapers; being a published poet; and writing the aforementioned manual. Now he is at work on one book about the first decade of the Dance Theatre of Harlem and another that will be a DTH cookbook.

The Shook odyssey came to rest in 1968 when Arthur Mitchell, who had retired from the New York City Ballet and founded the Dance Theatre of Harlem, asked Shook to return to the States as his co-director. Shook, who had always had ties with the ideals underlying the DTH, consented. It is likely he will remain for the foreseeable future, since, as he says, "When I was in Holland I felt that my work had to have something besides just rehearsing ballets and retraining dancers and so forth. I guess I was also searching for social, spiritual, and moral satisfaction." Has he found it? "Oh, yes! I couldn't ask for better." So it is possible that in the gypsy world of dance, DTH may be Shook's last and happiest stand.

Not long ago Adriano Adriana, a dance writer abroad, described Shook in print as "a genius teacher, if one ever existed." Another, Julian Tissot, said: "He is the scientific pedagogue and the perfect artist . . . a mesmerizing quietness. . . . For him the ballet classroom is a place of purification and preparation, and within its confines he presides as a dedicated priest." Still another, Paulina Grandi, said that Shook "brings to the classroom a serene magic."

They are all correct. The manner is the master. Shook has not visibly altered his principles in a decade. His craft was part of his marrow from the moment eyes ever lifted to stage. He is a monochromatic man in the sense of profound understanding of the bounty of history and total commitment to its transmittal. Not too much of what Shook says is new. But the fact of the utterance is, because, as he says, too many teachers pay only lip service to the verities, if they pay anything at all. They see in rote and technique the end-all, letting it end there, smug, satisfied, eyes turned the other way.

Shook understands that man's time on earth can be told as much in dance as in music, or perhaps more, and that from tribal village to polished ballroom the psyche is distilled and spirits assuaged. The humanity of this, and the science, are mixed in the retort of his mind and spread over the boys and girls in front of him and around him with infinite care to nurture and strengthen their emotions, learning, and total condition. Like Tevye, Shook believes in tradition with the positive assurance of right, and tradition is the figured bass of his teaching.

It is conceivable that one may successfully argue alternatives to Shook's pedagogy, but his philosophies appear unassailable. He has, for example, tremendous respect for his profession and for the student. Within an hour of first sight, he says, he has a fair idea what the student will be able to do, then and later—and he will not push. His lexicon of instruction is tempered in the crucible of experience. If he has something to work with, he goes to work, with a reason for everything. Many teachers talk too much and make corrections without respite, Shook says, and he is against that. The same teachers probably center their instructions on rules and routine, believing they cannot miss. In Shook's book they do.

The fact that Shook says the obvious ("The dance teacher must be involved with the total human being") is not the point. The fact that he believes it, is. And when his love is so deep that he is moved to write that dance is "a germinal force in mutual understanding, and therefore a potent instrument in the production of world peace,"* either he is gone on the subject and to be taken with a grain of rosin or he is a direct descendant of Noverre, Blasis, Cecchetti, and Vaganova, and needs to be heard with scrupulous attention. Guess which.

*Karel Shook. *Elements of Classical Ballet Technique: As Practiced in the School of the Dance Theatre of Harlem.* Dance Horizons, 1977, 81 pp.

*"Dancers as Ambassadors," *Unified World,* September 1978, pp. 3-9.

Left: Already soulful and lyric in demeanor, Muriel here is in a pose from her "fancy dancing" days just prior to auditioning for Anna Pavlova.

Below: Muriel Stuart, age four, spreading her wings on the verge of taking her first dance lessons.

Above: In the middle
1930s, when the School of
American Ballet was
located on Madison
Avenue. Photo by
Alexander Leber.

Left: An early studio portrait
of Muriel Stuart which she
is fond of and supposes
was taken in the early
1930s.

Left: At the Ida Winter Clarke School, Lake Charles, La., Muriel Stuart teaches as a representative of the School of American Ballet. Circa 1970. Photo by Fred Smith.

Below left: Although this photograph was taken in the early 1970s, Muriel Stuart looks much the same today.

Below: Teaching at the School of American Ballet. Photo by Martha Swope.

Right: At the School of American Ballet, when Stuart could not resist dancing along with her classes. Photo by Martha Swope.

MURIEL STUART travels in the best of circles. Also parabolas, arcs, and figures of eight. That is to say, she teaches in curves—seamless, indivisible, and full of grace. She did, after all, sit at the feet of Anna Pavlova and embrace her essence, and dance with her company, and she is another precious link with the Russian School and the golden past.

An erect, handsome, gray-haired woman with a slender figure and joyous face whose public persona is like a walk through Paradise Garden, Stuart today teaches two classes a week at the School of American Ballet.

A combination of dame, belle, duenna, and lady, Stuart teaches with the gentle authority of a classmistress shepherding girls across the lawn—a British lawn, to be sure. "Come along, someone, Come along with me. Come along, sweetheart, let's go! This way, my dear; try it this way. Sagging heels—watch out for that. Now, there's where your body should be!" as she floats from barre to barre in puffs of gentility and noblesse.

Stuart's manner is deceptive. Though somewhat softer than the iron hand in the velvet glove, she is no pushover. *Laissez faire* is not in her vocabulary. She remonstrates without bruising ego or hope, but remonstrate she does.

Her strength is in persistence and indirection—persistence in that her students are bound to absorb the lyricism that Stuart inherited from Pavlova, and indirection in that Stuart sugarcoats her commands with such skill that anyone younger than 22 is taken in, startled to find herself dancing correctly with perhaps no categorical idea of how she achieved that end.

Indirection may be an imprecise word. The lyricism of Stuart's world of dance is reflected in her teaching, and if she personifies politesse, abhorring violence, then that is her way. It merely seems like indirection, since she accomplishes so much with honey.

Her manner is no different in private conversation. She talks with animation about events long ago and far away, but to get underneath the skin and search for what moves Stuart today is difficult. One must read between the lines and closely watch her face, for she will put little that is substantive about her private world into words.

These facts, however, are ascertainable.

She was born in South Norwood, near London, and attended a "fancy dancing" class at the age of six. This was *de rigueur* at the time, and her two older sisters also were subjects. They turned out to be uninterested, but Stuart took to dancing. Her Austrian father and Scottish mother approved of the arts, which made it easier, and Mum even made her costumes.

"I enjoyed it all," Stuart recalls. "The boys wore white gloves, the girls pretty little dresses. We used to walk about the room with dumbbells in our hands, learning graceful movements and occasionally a simple waltz. The dumbbells were to develop the arms and chest, I think."

Two years later Pavlova announced from her home at Ivy House in London that she wished to teach and train eight girls who had had no prior experience. When it came Stuart's turn to audition, the child danced a waltz. Pavlova asked the pianist to segue into a polka—and so did Stuart, without notice, in response to the tempo change. This excited Pavlova's interest no end, since she was curious about the children's ability with rhythm.

"This striking, elegant woman so simply dressed, spoke quietly to me and asked me to stand in front of her. She wanted to see my feet, to see whether the arches were good. She examined me closely to see whether the body proportions were right, and then asked me to sit beside her while she auditioned the other girls.

"It was a great honor, and I felt quite hopeful, but several weeks went by without hearing whether I made it. Then the letter came giving us the good news and the date and time for the first lesson. She had never taught anyone before, and she was a hard teacher in the sense of making us repeat whatever we were doing until we got it right. But her patience was fantastic, no less than her poetry and artistry."

A lot of water has passed under the bridge since then, but Stuart returns to Pavlova again and again in conversation, for whatever the great ballerina gave her has survived the decades and remains the foundation of Stuart's craft.

Well, it is no mystery. In Pavlova's day technique was not the answer to everything. In fact, much technique was still being discovered. Pavlova's fame lay not only in dancing but in mesmerizing audiences by her acting. Most great Russian stars had the quality, but in Pavlova's hands it came out double-distilled. Watching Stuart in class (it is seldom possible to watch anyone else) one notes the Byronic position of the head, the languor of the arms, the scooping bend of the torso, the foot extended in narrow *pointe.* She is conveying to her students a legacy of yesteryear with only enough modern technique to make it work today.

When Stuart was 13 she entered Pavlova's company and performed with it for 13 years, until 1926. In the first how-to year she observed—how to walk, how to apply makeup—and appeared on stage briefly and in the rear. "It was my apprenticeship," Stuart recalls. "There isn't anything precisely like it today; there doesn't seem to be the time."

In 1926, Stuart married and went to live in San Francisco. She opened a studio there the following year and another in Los Angeles in 1931. She studied in both places with Harald Kreutzberg, who gave master classes in her studios whenever his tours took him to California. Having explored all manner of dance while with Pavlova it did not seem unusual to her, born and bred into ballet, to venture into modern dance, which in those years was the enemy camp.

"This is one thing about Pavlova that has never been brought out, that she was interested in every form of dance and all the other arts. We took lessons in Indian dance when we were in India. We took lessons in Japanese dance in Japan. She took us to see museums and exhibitions."

After the termination of her first marriage, and during her second marriage, and following the birth of her son Peter, Stuart studied dance with Carmelita Maracci, Martha Graham, and Hanya Holm, and dance composition with Louis Horst. It was at the suggestion of Agnes de Mille that Stuart was invited in 1934 to join the School of American Ballet. She was given the option of teaching whatever she wanted, but did not feel that she could presume to teach Graham technique or any other, and so returned to classical ballet. "It is really a Russian school, after all," she says.

"I must amend that somewhat," she added. "We did teach such things as character dancing and plastique. Plastique was a word invented to disguise what we call modern dance. It would not have done for a ballet school, you see, to have admitted to an acquaintance with modern dance."

In the early years Stuart taught three classes a day and was sent by the school to various parts of the country to assist in reinforcing the principles taught at the School of American Ballet. "Teachers would come to the school during the summers and watch Mr. (George) Balanchine hold classes. None of these teachers had students anywhere near so advanced as those in the school, so they asked whether we could visit their establishments, and teach, and help them and their students understand what was involved."

As the school grew, and as other teachers and disciplines were introduced, Stuart's schedule decreased as did those of her colleagues in order to make room for the new. In those years she preferred to teach beginners and intermediates, because "although very painstaking and slow, and requiring an enormous amount of patience, the placement of the body alone is so important. The shoulders have to drop softly down; the feet are in an unnatural position; movement has to be inspirational, and you can't give someone inspiration if she doesn't have a very fine, carefully coached foundation. The work with children is so interesting because you've got raw material, and you can enhance and enable it—open them up, so to speak, and let their souls come forth."

Stuart says she enjoys teaching more than she did performing. Early in her career behind barres when the spell of the stage still was upon her she would dance with her students—get in the front line before the mirror and dance out the combinations she had given them verbally a moment before.

She does much less of that now. She explains, but seldom demonstrates, and like nearly all her colleagues she explains almost sotto voce, accompanied sometimes by a flurry of hand signals which students, even when her back is turned, appear to receive. Her approach is still lyric, but the cantus firmus of her teaching is preparation of the body.

On this subject she is articulate. The years are wasted if technical preparation is not perfect to begin with. "It's a daily grind for them, I know, but thank heaven I've got more patience now and I understand my students better—what to do with them, how not to force the talented ones, how to prepare the positions, how to take care of each individual body. One other thing I have is a good ear. Movement must be motivated by the music, and the right kind of music is so important."

The music in Stuart's class is in many ways a reflection of her. The passages at the piano are a little bittersweet, a little poetic, a little romantic, sturdy in the middle but faded at the edges—not that Stuart is, of course, but the music does evoke bygones. So does Stuart. But curiously, for she is a modern woman in all apparent ways. It is in her teaching that she harks back to values once held. And similarly, the combinations she devises for her advanced class are just as low-key and softly diffused.

Her girls are generally excellent, and they catch her mood. She greets them wearing, unvaryingly, a long skirt, leotard top and bit of scarf about the throat. Her slippers are black with bright pink ribbons. If one judges by photographs she has worn the same outfit, top to toe, for years.

As she floats about, touching and correcting gently with love, now and then she will leave off and cruise the room snapping her fingers in time to the music. It is the sharpest sound one hears. Occasionally she throws a visitor the sort of sidelong glance that accompanies a rolling of the eyes, except that the eyes don't roll (no such *lèse-majesté*), and the glance is so fleeting as to be imperceptible.

After 45 years of turning students into dancers at the School of American Ballet, Stuart could be forgiven for being jaded. But no! Every day, she says, brings surprises and promises, and like the Good Fairy, she is eager to bestow her kiss.

HECTOR ZARASPE

Above: Early in his career as a teacher, a conventionally shorn Zaraspe (though already holding the baton that is his trademark) guides Vera Noralma, an Ecuadorian ballerina, in a Madrid studio, 1957. Photo by Aumente.

Left: With Margot Fonteyn in Panama, 1967.

Below: Hector Zaraspe and friends, Paolo Bortoluzzi (left) and Rudolf Nureyev.

Above right: Zaraspe makes a point with Russian prima ballerina Maya Plisetskaya, as Helen Atlas, publisher of *Dance News,* watches in a studio of the American Ballet Center, school of the Joffrey Ballet, 1968.

Below right: In Cologne, 1972, Zaraspe guides a class led by Henning Kronstam of the Royal Danish Ballet. Photo by Pieter Kooistra.

Left: The Maestro shares a light moment with Japanese ballerina Noriko Kubota at Ballet Théâtre de Française Nancy, 1978. Photo by Pierre Petitjean.

Middle: Zaraspe in his New York City apartment before a photograph of his beloved mother, Cruz, 1976.

Bottom: Teaching with the heart, "not the head," Zaraspe shows how it is done.

Right: Zaraspe, every inch the old maestro, teaching at the School of American Ballet.

ECTOR ZARASPE is such a charmer and speaks such fluently
fractured English that not until afterward does one comprehend one's
failure to comprehend the finer points that were discussed.

Thus it is not consistently possible to fix with assurance the statistical
minutiae of Zaraspe's career, particularly not when his warm manner,
disarming grin, and innocent face persuade a visitor that the mental block
is his own.

In class, however, no such dichotomy reigns. Zaraspe is the suzerain of
what he surveys and, as if to the manor born (which he was), wears the
mantle gracefully. He is gentle, quiet, purposeful without being pushy, and
changeful in humor so that all his afternoons are as those of a faun.

Zaraspe came to general notice through an anecdote in Margot Fonteyn's autobiography.* It developed, subsequently, that both Fonteyn and
Rudolf Nureyev solicited his instruction whenever proximity made it feasi-
ble to do so, meaning that whenever either was performing in New York it
was likely that Zaraspe's talents as a coach would be called upon. Nureyev,
in fact, engaged Zaraspe as coach and adviser for the film, *I Am a Dancer*,
in which he appeared in 1970. It is a measure of Zaraspe's engaging and

irrepressible personality that only seven years earlier, when they did not know one another, Zaraspe asked Nureyev for a pair of his ballet slippers (a traditional request from a fan), and Nureyev refused, according to Zaraspe, but reconsidered and gave the future teacher one slipper, signed.

The trio keeps in touch, and though professional contact has lessened with time, respect and friendship endure. Fonteyn wrote that in her view Zaraspe's major qualities were a communicable enthusiasm, perception of small details in style, and a variety of, and interest in, *enchaînements.* Zaraspe also demonstrates very effectively, Fonteyn said; he has a strong sense of music and rhythm, and he is responsible "for amusing comments and criticisms that make students at ease, and eager to do their very best for him."

Zaraspe testimonials are not hard to come by. Violette Verdy, who is unique in her own ways, recognizes the quality in others. When she was coaching with Zaraspe as a principal in the New York City Ballet, she remarked that in transforming human clay Zaraspe "never loses sight of respect and kindness. All of us, perhaps wounded by experience and confused as dancers within a complex society, seem to lose our standards and sense of perspective. Hector never lets you lose perspective. He keeps you balanced, and he does it with love which you can't help but redirect toward the dance. He will open up a role and show you the heart and soul of it, divinely, purely, classically."

Of Verdy, Zaraspe says: "Violette is one of my favorite friends and artists. I have only admiration and affection for her."

Zaraspe is president and chief executive officer of numerous such mutual admiration societies. He "loves" every professional he knows, and they reciprocate. It is difficult not to become personal with him. "I teach with my heart, not my head," he says, and although the closeness is personal without becoming intimate, Zaraspe nevertheless broadcasts warmth. This total sincerity is in part responsible for his success at the Juilliard School in New York City, where he is a faculty member, and for his desirability as a coach, teacher, and ballet master elsewhere.

The Juilliard administration permits Zaraspe to accept outside assignments. Since 1971, when he was appointed to the faculty, Zaraspe has worked during summers and other brief periods in Cologne, Hamburg, Amsterdam, Rio de Janeiro, Canada, and Caracas, where he was the original ballet master of Ballet International de Caracas.

Zaraspe's pre-pedagogical career is easily told. He was born in Aguilares, a village near Tucumán, Argentina, and learned about dancing from his father, a tenant farmer and folk dancer. The family moved to Buenos Aires when Zaraspe was 10. He began to perform in school folk festivals and took lessons in Spanish dance and modern dance. Four years later he was fortunate to cross the path of Esmee Bulnes, a master teacher trained by Cecchetti, Bronislava Nijinska, and Lubov Egorova, with whom he studied ballet for three years.

In 1949, at the age of 18, he was accepted into the opera ballet company of Teatro Colon, Buenos Aires, where he danced for three years and discovered that the qualities for a great dancer were not present in him. Besides, he liked to teach. In 1951, while still at the Colon, he started a school for youngsters unable to pay for lessons. Under his tutelage three children were soon good enough to be taken into the company—and he was on his way.

His way led to Spain. There he got to know three great Spanish dancers, Mariemma, Pilar Lopez, and Antonio, the latter becoming a great and good friend. Zaraspe gave class to their companies, staged festivals, taught movement, and toured with Antonio as a dancer and teacher. At the conclusion of a tour in 1964, Zaraspe found himself in New York City with his prospects temporarily suspended except for the name of Robert Joffrey, whom someone had described as the director of a fine school.

Zaraspe and Joffrey were taken with one another, and Zaraspe was engaged as a teacher. He remained at Joffrey's American Ballet Center for five years, later in the period also teaching the Harkness II Ballet Company. During this important span he coached Nureyev, Fonteyn, Maya Plisetskaya, Eleanor D'Antuono, Patricia Neary, and others, as well as choreographing for the New York City Opera and for films and musicals.

In 1971 Antony Tudor left the Juilliard faculty and recommended Zaraspe as his replacement. Zaraspe was appointed, and with the freedom and opportunity which now are his, Juilliard is likely to remain his base.

Given Zaraspe's ingratiating manner, flowing romanticism, and propensity for friendship, it is not surprising that he should be at the top of his profession. But he was at or near the top in his early thirties. How did a simple, uncomplicated farmer's son attain the heights so soon?

The reasons are reflected in his teaching. One is that, courtliness and poetic demeanor notwithstanding, Zaraspe has a sharp mind and an eye peeled for the main chance. He has swung rhythmically up the ladder, and no one can really say whether he is on the top rung yet. A second reason is that Zaraspe does have the goods. He is that rare bird, the truly intuitive teacher who knows the difference between right and wrong without having had much practical experience with either, who sprang full-grown from the brow of Terpsichore. Dance for him a role he has never heard of, and he will spot flaws instinctively, both in dancing and in choreography.

Also, he learns from those he coaches and is proud to say so. He is fond of declaring that he absorbed as much from Fonteyn and Nureyev as they from him. "Nureyev is my model, Fonteyn my muse," he says, beaming that he, the master, could lie at their feet just as they, for their part, looked into his soul as into a mirror.

Groping for words to express what he feels his kind of teaching is about, Zaraspe says: "When you are honest, and your feelings are authentic, students and stars both respect you. Today, learning the techniques of dancing is so difficult. You can have fantastic bodies in front of you, but to make them work for and give color to the music, give aristocracy to the music, what you tell them must be authentic.

"I was born with this feeling, I think, to express emotions freely with my body. I want to communicate to people what beauty is, and I think my spiritual gift gives me the authenticity of the beauty. Probably because I feel nature and life and God, this communication with others provokes something special, and they respect me and invite me to teach."

(Zaraspe is deeply religious. He wears about his neck a sculptured gold-and-silver Cross, a gift from Ghislaine Thesmar, ballerina of the Paris Opera Ballet. He speaks of ballet, religion, and the Deity in the same breath, and often.)

"You have to represent the art of the dance spiritually first and combine with the body and communicate to the students what dance is. It comes from inside the body. What I try to tell my students is that everybody has something to give, but you have to grow up inside, and this goes for poets, painters, musicians, actors. I say to my students that you have to give the same thing with your body, you have to frame music with your body, you have to give poetry with your body. . . ."

Colorful, voluble and social outside the classroom, inside the sacred precincts Zaraspe addresses his students quietly, with a faraway look. His speech is soft, his accents sweet, and he is in control. In the relationship of coaching, Zaraspe's manner may seem to an onlooker to be less bemused as he delivers instruction and ignites understanding with a sure tongue and courage backed by authority. He does not hesitate to tell superstars where and how they err, and what to do about it. They accept without exception, since his version of truth invariably is synchronous with their instinctive, if inarticulate, own.

Zaraspe teaches no particular style. He is apt to enfold elements of Cecchetti, Vaganova, Volkova, and Messerer in his exercises, but basically his goals are "clean movement and coordination of body and mind. Emotions and the physique have to be together. Tender is tender, but you can complicate it with another step, another movement. Simplicity is the key to beauty. For that I try."

When he can, he audits the classes of other teachers, all of whom he "loves," in order "to learn from them." In that he is quite sincere. He is not trying to pick their brains, but to remain *au courant* on the road to truth, beauty, and the rainbow. Nonetheless, because of his reputation, one would imagine his colleagues must surely become unsettled as he inserts himself unobtrusively into their classrooms.

Most teachers promote student exposure to museums, theater, literature, music, and the arts in general. While Zaraspe has no objection, for him instinct and intelligence are the operative words. They explain why he is in such demand, and his reputation so high, with comparatively little formal training behind him. Zaraspe goes by what his antennae tell him, and their messages—born of instinct, shaped by intelligence, and filtered through the fine mesh of good taste—emerge as pictures from an exhibition of his soul. He stakes his career on them.

It should be mentioned that Zaraspe still is a choreographer of respectable attainment. His works—good enough to deserve repetition—often appear in recitals of the Juilliard Dance Ensemble. They have flair, variety, and a touch of the poet. His magnum opus may well be a ballet that has not yet seen studio lights. He calls it *Juana La Loca* and has written the libretto, whose choreography he hopes will be done by Antonio. Juana was the daughter of Isabella La Catolica, the Spanish queen who sent Columbus to the west, and Juana later went mad with love—for her husband, of all people.

Good idea, no? Zaraspe wrote it as a tribute to Fonteyn, who liked the libretto, he says, and who at one time might have danced it. He sees *Juana La Loca* as a film to be made in Spain, "and if Margot cannot do it I will have to talk to another ballerina."

The true balletomane believes that the female dancer, with turned-out feet that make her waddle, skin stretched tight on her bones so that no voluptuary would consider her twice, with hair drawn into a chaste bun and her horizon as narrow as her waist, is the most beautiful and desirable of women.

Zaraspe, who is on familiar terms with lots of these beauties, might be expected to have a favorite whom he has coached. Tactful, gallant, and slippery as always, Zaraspe says: "All dancers are like flowers, and flowers have beautiful perfumes. In particular I love roses, and roses have most lovely perfume of all. And some of my dancers are like roses, yes?"

---

*Margot Fonteyn. *Autobiography*. Knopf, 1976, 266 pp.

AFTERWORD

IF ONE RECOGNIZES a similarity among the teachers presented here, one is correct. Certain verities are shared, such as discipline, respect for the individual, worship of total culture, and the basic training of good habits.

In each instance, however, there is something more. Most teachers are specialists—one in *pointe* work, another in the classic manner, a third in adagio, and so on. Still, they always insist that, particular expertise notwithstanding, all students could expect to receive a well-balanced education at their hands—and that is true.

Yet the alert student and established performer know through the grapevine who is especially good at what, and they drift. They will leave Madame X for Maitre D, because Madame may be good in port de bras but not in allegro. Similarly, some may use their faculties to leave one school and sign up at another because at the first one they were unhappy in love while at the other there is hope in strengthening the arch.

Reasons need have nothing to do with logic. Dancers and would-be dancers live ephemeral lives structured on emotion and unreality. But they are monomaniacal in their direction—straight up. They are ridden by intimations of their own mortality; in few other professions is there such singleness of purpose.

The greatly talented have a stage life of perhaps 25 useful years; all others, a decade less; and wasting time is anathema. Thus, dancers who owe their training to a single teacher are rare. They go where they can get what they imagine to be the best training, so that they may be launched in prime time—say, at 16 or 17.

Master teachers are forsaken fewer times than their colleagues because they have the skill and wisdom to offer more and because the more altruistic among them occasionally nudge their best students elsewhere if the going should be good.

Nonetheless, a teacher does yearn to be able to point with pride and exclaim with an effort at modesty, "Yes, she's mine from the start!" Most are aware, however, that all is vanity, that the deep inner satisfaction of having contributed at least to a piece of the action is fame enough. The proof will out. History will know.

INDEX

INDEX

Boldface numbers indicate pages with illustrations; a lower-case c after a page number refers to a caption.